THE PROFOUND M

To Tess Taylor –
a much admired
poet & friend
xo
T

2 Aug 2021

The Profound M

Poems by
Tamsin Spencer Smith

Photos from the collection of
Matt Gonzalez

San Francisco, California

© 2021 Tamsin Spencer Smith

Introduction by Matt Gonzalez

All rights reserved

ISBN-13: 978-1-7362624-3-6

"That do not do the thing that most do show" first appeared in the digital journal OmniVerse #84 on September 1, 2019. "Deep Song" first appeared in Issue 6 of Volume Poetry online on June 15, 2021.

Our thanks to Guy Diehl, who did the scanning and image preparation for the book, and to Angela Auyong, who prepared images for earlier proof versions. We are grateful to RiskPress Foundation for making the Divers Collection possible.

Since this project began, some of the photographs have been gifted to friends, including Donald Bradford (pg. 142), Lisa Chadwick (pg. 104), Guy Diehl (pg. 28), Alicia Escott (pg. 46), Ali Fenn & Rachael Lamkin (pg. 30), Carolyn Ji Jong Goossen (pg. 166), Tony Hall (pg. 138), Barry McGee (pg. 154), Michelle & Emilio Villalba (pgs. 42 & 182), Glynn Washington (pg. 120), and Cate White (pg. 144).

Author photo by Una Ryan

San Francisco, California

*Surrealism will usher you into death, which is a secret society.
It will glove your hand, burying therein the profound M
with which the word Memory begins.*

André Breton

NEVER LOST
Reflections on the Art of Found Photography

Memory, which André Breton referred to as the *Profound M*, is the thread that consistently runs through the vintage snapshot photos in this book. These images trigger a compelling nostalgia. They unexpectedly connect us to the original subjects by virtue of a shared cultural experience. Despite not being directly related to our own personal histories, we've all gone fishing, or goofed off with friends at a wedding, or tried to hold a handstand in the sand at the beach. Even if we haven't, we can still imagine that we might have, if given the chance. Thus, our memories become intertwined with these moments from someone else's past.

Of course, these photographs are only "found" insofar as they have been dispersed after the original owner of the keepsakes, or the families who treasured them, were no longer able to store them safely. Set adrift by the happenstances of life — relocations, broken marriages, natural calamities, or even death — they've weathered estate auctions and storage locker misadventures to become lost relics picked through at a flea markets or garage sale. When we say found photography, we are essentially speaking of the recovery of otherwise discarded or unclaimed family mementos.

The original photographer, almost always unknown to us today, likely prized these images as defining personal artifacts. Even a snapshot taken hastily during a vacation would be returned to again and again in the ensuing years, evoking a remembrance of things, places, people, and events past. Once archived in photo albums, they would become talismans, integral to an individual or group's perception of themselves. Memories not captured on film would fade far more quickly than those given outsized importance simply by virtue of having been preserved on film.

Sometimes these photos emphasize the mundane; a quick click of the camera while the subject was unawares. Other times, the protagonists strike a pose, one they might not have assumed had the camera not been aimed in their direction. As the presence of a camera can literally make things happen, it's hard to separate a moment from the way in which it is portrayed on film. Sometimes it's the photos that capture nothing much at all happening that pull the viewer in and spark the greatest possibilities for reflection.

Discussion with other collectors has fostered my belief in the value of these found photographs as contemporary art objects. Robert Flynn Johnson, curator emeritus of the Achenbach Foundation for Graphic Arts at the Fine Arts Museums of San Francisco, has published two important volumes of found photography (*Anonymous: Enigmatic Images from Unknown Photographers*. Thames & Hudson, 2004 & *The Face in the Lens Anonymous Photographs*. University of California Press, 2009). Johnson has noted in conversation that some of the particularly enigmatic photos survive because past generations revered the new technology of photography so much so that throwing away even bad photos seemed wasteful. It would have been counter to their frugal post-depression mindset to trash even the bungled shots. As a result, the choice to save outtakes allows a contemporary re-engagement with those errors. The artistic success of a partially overexposed, out of focus, or poorly cropped photo may now be considered as strikingly evocative because they couldn't have been posed and perhaps can't ever be replicated. Some of the best photos, those with the most intriguing and enduring aesthetic value, are the mistakes.

The Kodak Brownie, which is often credited as the original snapshot camera, made this technology accessible to hundreds of thousands of people. Although Eastman Kodak produced the first pocket cameras in the early 1890s, it wasn't until the release of the less expensive Kodak Brownie that photography became accessible to a wider audience. Invented by Frank Brownell and introduced in 1900, the Brownie was a cardboard box camera with a meniscus lens that took square 2 ¼-inch inch photographs. Later models were made of bakelite and had improved lenses. Kodak's early advertisement slogan emphasized how easy it was to use: *You Press the Button, We Do the Rest.*

While earlier pocket models were 5 times the price, the Brownie cost $1 ($30 in 2020 dollars), when first released. This affordable means of bringing photography to the masses was evidenced by the over 100,000 sold in its first year of production. Suddenly, everyone became an artist, even if their intent was more prosaic.

Later technology brought other innovations. The first widely distributed photo booth is credited to Russian emigree Anatol Josephewitz and appeared in New York City in 1925. For a single quarter, the device developed and printed eight photos in roughly 10 minutes. It was said to be so popular that over 250,000 people utilized the booth in its first six months. Capitalizing on its appeal, the Photomaton Company quickly distributed the new phenomena nationwide.

Polaroid's first commercially-available instant camera, the model 95 Land Camera, came out in 1948. For the first time, more personal or intimate photos could be had without an embarrassing trip to the developer. Photos capturing nudity and drug paraphernalia became something that people, who didn't have their own dark room, could generate themselves.

Found snapshot photography — sometimes referred to as "vernacular photography" by collectors — underscores that these photos often capture every-day, ordinary domestic moments. The sheer banality represented in some of these pictures is part of the special allure. With today's social media, snapshots are ubiquitous, even those depicting random quotidian moments. Pressure to invent our lives and portray what may be faux happiness or stylized perfection results in most perceived errors getting deleted. This is one of the things that makes the vintage photographs, and their second life as art objects, so special.

These brief moments in time are augmented here by Tamsin Smith's beautifully evocative poems. They are not meant to be literal, as if describing the action of the photograph; in fact, they would fail if they were to try. The poems offer a fresh way of looking at the photographs, an entry way into viewing their hidden mysteries. Since the meanings in the original photographs are nearly entirely obscured to us, Smith's poetry suggests new narrative possibilities and alternative histories. In effect, Smith is taking her own snapshots through the medium of words, mixing in the material of her own stories and imagination. I see this foremost as a book of verse, accentuated by the inspiration of persons long gone, who captured and cherished poignant moments, just as we do today.

The photographs in this book come out of a larger collection I have assembled over the years. Some were found at flea markets, bookstores, and even found littered on city streets. Many were purchased directly from the dealers who have nurtured a sizable community of snapshot photography collectors. Robert Jackson, whose exceptional collection was exhibited at the National Gallery in Washington, D.C. in 2007, in a show titled: "The Art of the American Snapshot, 1888–1978: From the collection of Robert E. Jackson," is the source of many of the photos contained herein. My gratitude is extended to him for his role in elevating these photographs into the American art cannon and encouraging my own engagement with them.

All but three of the photographs are anonymous. The exceptions are from Smith's and my own family collections. Augmenting the grouping in this way makes the finished product even more personal for us and links the book to the 1977 Scrimshaw publication, "American Snapshots, Selected by Ken Graves & Mitchell Payne", which I believe to be one of the earliest books featuring snapshot photography. That publication presented vintage snapshot photography chosen from family photo albums around the United States.

I have tried to include a variety of art forms here: the photo booth picture, the Polaroid, and even hand-colored photographs. What they share in common is that they make us ponder our own lives, working as springboards to our own memories, profound and otherwise.

Matt Gonzalez
San Francisco, CA

THE PROFOUND M

LADY OF THE LAKE

Here goes nothing
Hands in practical prayer
Pierce the flat forbidding
Surface of a life measured
By lossless splashes
Mess made versatile
By one's own design
Articulated jackknife
Split even the tree line
You will surrender nothing

MAY • 58 •

A PALO SECO

Luck shows
Her starfish
Hand glimmering
Fan of hemlock fire
Rotation of a southern tell
Rendezvous: plunge and suit
There at the monture
A bone parts
The queen's motif
Moves a scarlet gem
Jokers smiles his
Anemone ante
The sting
Of a single heart
Face up

WEIGHT

Is this what they mean those songs
That say balls in the air but beware
The surface shadow slows...

                         Wait for it,

The lift will happen naturally
Catch the cooler color down
A longer path. The 2x life
Perplexes machinery. Light even,
And the story falling through

OMNIFORMED

Square thoughts
Quilted by the blur
Of flashing fields

One station becomes
Another face-to-face
I wander in lost compartments

Questions about direction
The volatility of detail
Crouched in plain and plainer view

What gives it all away
As a doe the absence of antlers
Anthers of a more perfect flower

GRAND CANYONS

Those were the days

We reached

Without need

Typecast landscapes

Lavished hour upon hour

Far from our falls

Knees skinned yet

Never to utter a sound

Adieu too another

Arm of gestural greeting

Oak and pine

Green proverbs

Truth seen through

This war of skin

Beyond the sun's

Unwaged retreat

VIEW OF THE UNBROKEN COLUMN

Your secret thoughts

Strung as planetary baubles

The everything about you looks

Deeply patterned but your own

Broadest moment far beyond

Vincent, Frida or Hiroshige

Compass point

Your eyes steady

All that you behold

CALLOW YOUTH

On the lawn in your underwear
Reverie with cigarette
Arrested by a toad
Forever caught
In a metaphor
And a stranger's
One at that
Still
Here we are
What I wish
To transfer is
The toad alone
Replaced in the pocket
Of an impish pageboy
His dungaree overalls
And best mate beside
Sheltering the secret
Of hidden mischief
As if no one ever died

RACOON IN THE OLD GROVE

The afternoon you tried on
Your mother's dress and cut

Your fringe so close to show
You too could change spots

Just like the frogs that used
To be tadpoles stepped forth

From the pond beyond the sliding
Glass window to the golden world

Of nature where your father was
Most — with himself — less alone

Is the answer to why you did not play
With dolls but loved animals
Collected coins not candy on halloween
So proud of your unicef box and badge

And the poem a man will write
One day to assure you
He sees you standing there

WINTER BIRD

Slim and bright you surely glide
high above your own shadow

Cool sand and crossed paths
bead the skirts of a Cinderella sun

When I am not busy forgetting to feel
I sing your song
I think   I make no noise

But look
Stars have laced the air

This is how
      (through glass)
again
you will find me

WITH FEET TO FOLLOW

First

Under

Cover

Lovers

& Now

Forever

Friends

Watching

The days

Dip sweet

And slowly

ATLAS

There you go
Older than now
Tossing the how-to
Showing me your
Shoulders bear less
Great weight your gaze
Directly true holds
The dense smallness
& immense avowal of Today
Hoisted like a prize life
To be claimed

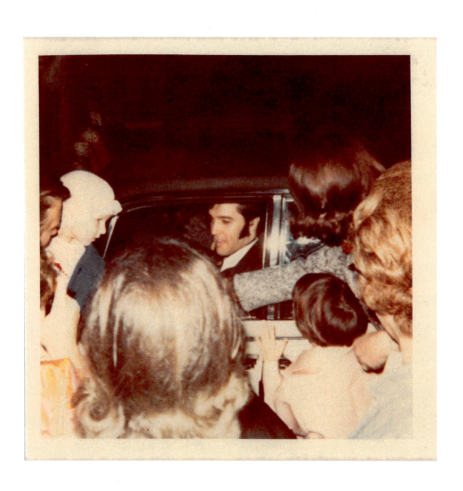

THE KING

In the official history of Britain
No magician taught the young son
Of Uther Pendragon
How to swim like a carp
Or fly like a hawk
As no one explains
That a man sometimes does good
Not because he is good but because he is not
And knows enough to wish it were not so
Despotic the Destiny we seek or the ways we
Escape what the soul of the man might say
To the image of the same
Loose hips, crooked lips
This is, a song for another day

PURIM PARTY IN AN UNKNOWN YEAR

On a day of deliverance
There will be feasting and gifts
For the poor who await their own
Little ray of sunshine in the clutch
Conceding escape from the masquerade
When boy-girls sprout petals
Girl-boys pledge miracles
Disguised as natural events
These legends keep us guessing
Anonymous almighty mystery
Those ageless pleading eyes

THE JOUST

Know ye damsel of any quests needing done
Might is in the world and this day makes one
Ride through the idiom of contradictions
Steamed to the stepped field with black fury
Forgetful even of the eaves, the scorched lawn
Unwatered, the soiled dishes I have left behind

RALIQUEST

Everywhere ice cubes

The jangle of heavy metal

Destiny like a prow of the boat

Hosted trampoline. Pick up!

We are forming a band

Unknown to teethless people

We are starting a march!

Drum it on a hot hood

On a hot belly

Briefs drawn down in dust

I can still feel the sugar pouring

The damnable luck of it all, this infinite

Everyday especially freedom, etcetera

ANOTHER CURE AT TROY

I don't wish to wake you

With abrupt stories

Let me observe

The human body in sleep

So vulnerable to centuries

Of anonymous dreams

Rocked in the cradle of animal tracery

Division divided from its shell

Of pawprint, wing, and star trail

Bright behind black lashes

Lullabies at dawn

Leaned against you

Seeking warmth

ALSO THE DRAGON EARTHBORN

Preacher boy and me
Skip stones in the cemetery
Count eleven ways of getting lost
Just one for breaking free
Took his case to the city
Sold his hat and grew his hair
That metal vault I coiled inside
You'll find his slingshot there

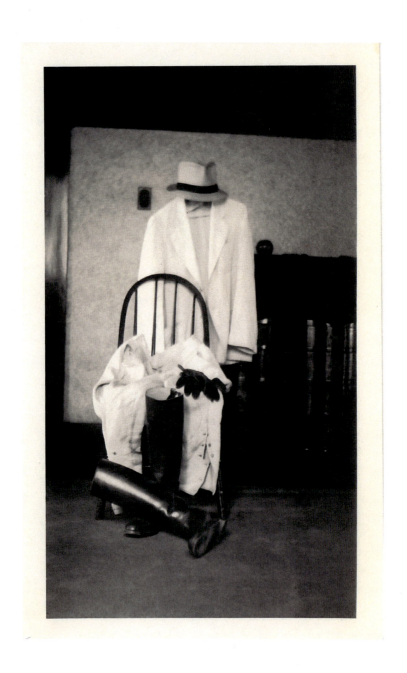

INTERIOR GEOMETRIES

Due to movement and long exposure
Time makes a merger of blurred faces
And surroundings get obscured become
Memories more of possibility than fact
The empty gloves, the banded hat
I lie naked in the bedroom waiting

THE TURN

It was 1973 & we runway
Kids were winning our own perfect season
The skyline sprang steely with twin pillars
To thrust some kind of victory on high Heaven
& the dirtiest president of the day cast
His first of many backward goodbyes
From a speed boat on the Biscayne Bay
But the snowstorm hadn't yet hit our island
We'd be all rainbow sleek and glossy lipped
Hit what lay before there even was a Studio 54
Listen to Liza belt it out and pray
Josephine Baker's coming home today
To turn cartwheels in her cuffs and pearls
Teach strangers to clap and stare
Slow vamp turns on a double dare
Mon ange coloré
When you varnish the night
The whole sky arches beneath
We used to wear our poems so tight
Anyone could tell
Just by looking

SHIFTED BY DROPS

Slick camouflage
Outbraved grace
Against temptation
Sits the set of her
Pearl sharp teeth

STAR OF VENUS

Fizz over flute rim

What god would set you

Out to spring no less

Kept that copper dry & lit

Westerly prophesies

Poured in eights

Single hose

Back turned

Engine running

AWAKE! AWAKE!

Those in search of the way
        miss the true nature of self   Be
            not fooled by the relative mind
Many
forms   fit
        as a means of discipline
used to admonish
            the first mask
stares into the bottom   of the water

gourd
the bark cloth
the pith of certainty
                yield
    Brick Red Boos + Acid Green Predominate

PEEK A BOO

You walk tall and carry
the biggest wand you can
find among the cast off
circuitry of modern cities
to shake the unknown stories
of a once-native species saved
by bobbling bottles and sunken
chests – a mopping up of mess
and miles of love letters – where
merely human once claimed dominion
she now there lives a keeper of dreams

UNDER MY SKIN

We met in the soft dry grass
Behind the dunes beyond the summer
Seasoning the metaphysics of anatomy

Traced the tertiary tensions
Where touch and temperature solicit
Sensations rapidly slide in scale

Did my being soprano green
Take anything higher or deeper
When each life is a said verb

Be one gesture
Wordless confession
Leaf and hope

ALL SORTS PLUS WEATHER

We were not made
To cover mouths
Hands having many
Better maneuvers
& here's where I gather
Then pause behind my filter
To consider the meaning of safety
In the slender stalk of your neck
Pure white swan of coy permission
Fairytales and public parks happily
Belonging ever after assured
Though no one wants to fight
We do not see your fists but hope
Perhaps they clench beyond
Our view and your own story
Simmer for the unquenched
Characters of shared history

A PERSISTENCE OF MEMORY

So much felt pressure
Hedges line the horizon.
A pied flatness stands two-
Leveled, well-balanced at least
The train tests reality as it is
draped and long skirted
whistles to itself. What of it,
where's to look? One wind up
lever clocks the minutes
of a certain striding poise.
Ear to the ground. Slower
Dragging of the gaster.
This is verse versus propulsion:
Arms, legs
In theory, at ease
The midday air could
Rid us of dull history
Make metaphysical things
Of tin and temperance how
Each of us longs to be held

PATIENCE

The day's most minute gift
Counts its change
Dares you to pluck a daisy

Give this promise your most
Immediate attention
As window at high noon

May nothing distract you
From the consequence of acceptance
What lags behind this porous vigil

OCTOBER 1969

A supersonic jet tested the air above our heads
As an explosion 4,000 feet beneath the sea caused
The dome of the earth to rise and send some lakes
Sky high while an aspiring star leapt to her death
The news called it suicide but her dad the tv host
Railed against LSD and introduced america
To a troop from old blighty whose flying circus
Had nothing to do with the weather underground
Or soviets in space nor the largest protest yet
Against the war of the silent majority upon the general
Sanity of the people and fans who would see the Mets win
And here the cheer *Sugar, Sugar* by the Archies relieved
To learn that Paul was still alive and living in Scotland...

HALF-UNWORTHY, HALF-DIVINE

The altered line can liberate experience
Things emerge from actions taken
This may sound theoretical
I know you prefer the black and white
Of what was or was not meant
Yet intention gets frayed and fades
Each lost second a new essence formed
Fractional fusions of farewell and forever
Think your mad career of broken barriers
Missing the idle laps to come

WOMEN

No less a refuge

In roseate particles we

Bloom laughter as the world

Wings towards its own toothy togetherness

Are we not sisters to the soul

Oblivious to gravity

Giggling at grass snakes

Sable grey fences

WINGS OF DESIRE

Paging the faded
Regular shapes
[cornered small black brackets]
Whose glue has long since
Ceased to hold their quarry
You leap ^ O instantaneous you
Peg pushed against shadow
2 points + more revelations
About angels

COCONUT GROVE

In the land of the actual palm
And expanse of half-loud youth
We ended everyday upside down
In water painted blue by plastic bobbing birds

The sun we saw lived below the water line
Planting thoughts we liked whistling
I remember feeling close and how
I'd make a parasol of fronds to twirl

Toes apoint
The sky abyss
Synchronized by
Artful consequence

GO FISH

Can't see yours
But barefoot
I'd have been
Cat-scratched
Bug-juiced
Arms across a melon
To test the weight
Of making
Imaginary friends
Might we also climb
Trees to spy on neighbors
And barter live worms
Hooked by laughter

COVER GIRL

The struggle to be
Always has been
Even more so perhaps
In the age of gloss

Face of a woman sheered
Of the divine actual
Freckles and baby fat flattened
Fictions of perfect composure

You may have been playing
Among alabaster statuary
Shy to the camera and hidden
Behind what was handed down

But your warm brown limbs
Reveal where beauty originate
Elbows and a mind that knows
Pages don't turn themselves

THE EMPRESS OF FAIRY FLOSS

When did you last taste
Excitement towering over
The imagination filled
In a way that fostered
Fantasy however slight
Some turn of battle
A victorious excess
All is not lost &
Discovery, shores
Of seamless dreaming
Days without doors

FIESTA DE DULCES

Break the new year
As a clay idol covered
In feathers with your
Sticks of many colors
Blind but festooned
Sweet treats will fall
Before you like rain

MOVING DAY

Star fish the size of cabbages
Washed ashore the summer
We met and fell in love
Cleaving to each look
Or touch my skin did
Burn. Did yours? You
Never said but kept
This tucked away
Between pages
Of an old book
That logged
Appointments
You set in a pile
Marked *KEEP*

PACIFIC THEATER

Summer camp
Canoe prank
I'll be the shark fin
You be the life saver
We'd met in older years
A band of brothers on
A distant lapping shore
We watched an island mother give birth
Where sand slopes to the innocence of ocean

SEMAPHORE

Suppose you'd have been a baby then
Pulled from the nursery for disturbing
The other children on board ship while
U-Boats circled Ring around the Rosie
Your mother sang in a language she
Had just begun to speak and no flag
Much less two to wave together
Not to surrender but to signal
Peace as visible

COLOPHON

Sea lily fossil
Difference is a kind
Of suddener sameness
Warm world, please with your
Paralleled percentages
& finishing touches
Words that begin with L
End me in growth + multiples
The placing of one's mark

THAT DO NOT DO THE THING THEY MOST DO SHOW

Tumble weed

Cannon ball

Desert wind

Burn

Hot pitch

Quickdraw

When your back is turned

Telephone to back home

Three stripe to knee

Reptile road trip

Temptation follows me

 (stone teeth,

       with small arms extended)

RASPBERRY HUMINGBIRD SUNDOWN

Friendship is not a countable thing as a list of favorite songs or places we hope to visit. It's a small porous sachet tied to the end of the smallest finger on our non-dominant hand, in which a rainbow composed of twigs from no tree we've ever known appears. And we are there.

LONELY IMPULSE OF DELIGHT

The night grows mauve
Eighth moon in the open
Orchard quavering
Sleep-sewn veils
Pitched to the thief of air
Schools of silvery fish
Flit but do not suspect
They have been wished upon
Thus this will be a battle
Transformed by bright-edged
Ellipses beading the wing
Here the stars are ravishing
Partaken of the night

PILGRIM

Dive in and into that ocean
You will know another carriage
In the manner of air cooling scales
Awaiting the slap of fish flying, of banners
A veil torn by the fast-rushing current
Angles an iridescence forever patterned in
Patience a clue to understanding when
Some magnificent silence proclaims
Here

LOCKET

Darling, to bed
Twilight tumbles
Thick between the folds
You making dawn to me
Me making dawn to you

ROADSIDE ATTRACTIONS

Dive in

Drive by

Dream on

Keeping it

Real cool thru

Day turns at dry noon

THE LIONESS DISPATCHES

A soul editor so grand
As to be invisible
Devoted to infinitives
Unsplit by bylines
Bored and belted
Shall not miss the point
Of my pencil's purpose
Marking a submission box
Does not square a cylinder
Or teach the hyena grammar
Manners used to have a syntax
Like word-given parentheses
It's time you learned to behave

FIGUREHEAD

To the end you have traveled a lark in flight
As a trumpet of secondary senses, a keepsake
Of comings that never fall to earth, an unlikely
Universal flare, a mirror mirroring the first leap

Before the big splash

BEFORE THE BIG SPLASH

Whoever may be listening
This is my master class in perfection, go
Straight armed and miles long before we let up
Make way many molecules more will follow
There's a planet carries these names
A constellation in which every star is our
Worlds so big within us

A SHARED COLLECTION

In the plein air painting of our life, love
There will be a gentle curve and invitation
To horizon beyond the well-marked guard
Rail. You might picture me as Grace
Kelly with a long scarf flowing
The sound of Satchmo prompts you
To tease me about being so grand
But what I'd actually like to say
Is that this I'm not done looking at you

EQUINOX

What can you believe of an event
So hot and violent that light could not pierce
Until we expand and get cool

All moments are
Chances flashing
Until I interrupt you

THE FRIENDSHIP GALLERY

Remember the party where we all wore hats
From your collection and raised our glasses
As lights played patterns across the bridge
Span and practically swam over so as not to miss
The toasts and simply just to feel the glow that had
Nothing to do with candles but everything to do
With the strike of lightning and the stroke of luck
And the day you were born, which still is the best
Thing about winter and wow I just learned yesterday
You wanted to be a welder making art on the street
To please all the people passing by and now I can see
Small gold circular boxes made by pressure melding
Lap joints or intricate hammer-formed iron arcs to remind
Us all that the best of what's to come awaits so here's
To next and to always and to the links that set us free

EXPOSURE

Picked from the pile

Of covered up

Or cut away

A defaced stare

The letter left unsent

Emotion's floating asterisks

An answer without a question

For all of our instants held

Too long or not enough

RISKING BREAKAGE

She closed the book and called
To the stones overhead
Catch me if you can

VAST GLOWING

A lot of this empty bliss

Beyond the backyard

Awaits my arrival

I'm an unlit match

Ready to strike

EVER AFTER

Sprawling branch slows the sun
Summer rides its mother's tide
Typical birds cry their particular news
"I cannot answer for the chestnuts"
Squirrels shrug
A spoke of toothed leaves turns
To the blushing blueberry
Dark unreadable pages
Wet with juice

DANGEROUS CONDITIONS

I'd rather be the train hauling
Rocks up steep terrain than a tree
Rolled on a river and ridden down
Stream. I'd rather drown a letter left
Unfinished than pick burrs
From a steamy drain.
I cover your eyes
Then mine
Free again
(free again)

PALE RIDER

The hope of those years
In flight from a warring
World sunk to save itself
In stove top ovens and
Lawnmower cowboys

TRANSMISSION

Been speaking to trees
Beating the code of bark
Against an inner drum
Slurring apology
To the undergrowth
Walking through brick
Walls on my knees
Thick and thankful
I had forgotten
This secret speed
Of spore and season
Old stand and savage bud
Blurred by each new leaf

SNAP

An in-the-moment myth
of the bird child born between
verticals. You carry the chorus
for those who stood tall before you.
Then one warm afternoon in the park
When they said you couldn't dance
I felt the shame of just listening
wanting to roll back the story,
the clock, run in and object
But that just proves the broken truth
Of how the wind blows different
On the same flame but we know
Which wishes work the wonders
In the end you got the winning moves

ENDLESS SUMMER

The geometry of glee
Sand and steep angles

Horizon rises clean against
Gravity and light loss

We pretend not to hear
The bell so hard to touch

BUFFALO NICKEL

The red rum resisted
The ice bucket ran
Away with you, sun
And we'll sink another
One down the slot
To make the bed
Shake indistinctly
Rubbing out years
Like the last two
Lately minted

FISH STORY

You'd speak of the lake
As if it were the one link left to your family
The bragging father with his buckshot politics
Mother of martinis, bridge, and false laughter
A child's faith in the absurd but endearing
Is a form of legacy, a lesson in collation
You'll say that forgiveness was never the point
We must focus on the object in your hands
Not the other eyes watching
In order to fully weigh
The actual size of anything

THE GOOD YEAR

A new bud shoulders
The spent flower
Blows it away
Like the kiss
We'll call
A poem

ART

We come into this world
Laden with this world
Like a pond full of fish
You must not deny me
Parables, hope, or erosions
Thereof but simultaneously
The first and lastness of us
Moving together like water

TOTEM

Monumental carvings depict
Whole histories of culture and clan
How Raven owed a debt and Kats
Won the bear woman but lost his way
In the woods no one now remembers
Or the park which framed the free fact
Worlds grow weightless without boundary

PROPHESY

Imagine in the graced

Light of an ancient August

Your feet washed by bayou

Argentine sand and Spanish moss

Hothouse vines obscure the conscious

Mind your wild and curious twin returns

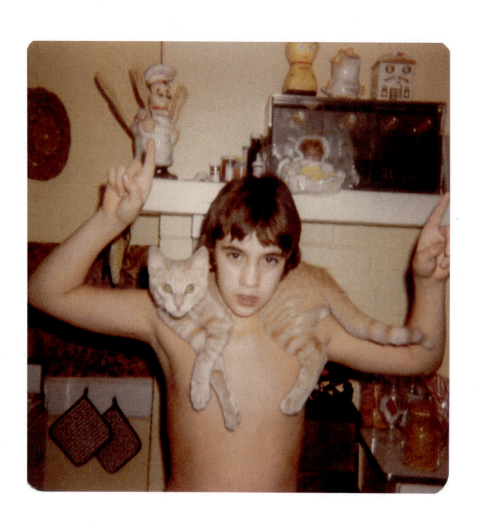

FAUN'S AFTERNOON

Always the exquisite thought emerges
Marx and Mallarme from the crockery

There is a reason that poets give homage
to wild creatures. Do you remember

how fur felt against
your ardent young chest?

THE BANDLEADER OF BANTRY BAY

Oh, could I lope me long in her grassy coves
hear the baritone rolls of the celtic sea
— but that pleasantest shore is far from
this tour; I got prairie dust under my feet.

The crowds come for more of my full-throated
roar and the tunes that old blue eyes sang neat —
Shake my boxer's paw and admire this jaw
that took rounds with Muhammad Ali.

Call me Antelope Jack or Desert Hare
but don't follow too close on my tail —
For I'm hopping the fence and legging it
Soon to return to the green isle of Bere.

LION OF THE SUBDIVISION

How bright was your mind
Teeming behind the quiet
Steady eyes in an era
Said to be simpler
Simply for having
Cleaner streets
Meaning less
Material to
Assemble
Into art

TAG

Climbed everything we could
Braver than army ants we spat
At killer bees tossing our crusts
High above the gum trees hoping
The wrens could catch them
Midair –and never miss a beat
With wing-sky-tree-body
We used to know our own
Speed – said we'd never
Slow down
Except…
You're it!
…for ice-cream

NEIGHBORLY

So and so works the grill
Tragic and beautiful sunflowers
Hold out their cocktails to the warm
Gingham god of summer waiting to be called
On and on goes the carousel of sensory
Recall looking for places to slip
Around the standard fixings

TRAVELING THROUGH THE DARK

The call and response of childhood
Knock knock   Or have you heard
The one about the people you're not
To call anymore or the phrase
That says your words don't hurt me
Though sticks and stones sometimes do
And surely this reader knows the joke
Of the pacifist poet sent to a camp
For conscientious objectors where
They taught each other what they knew
Now they're still publishing those verses
Long after their deaths prove history does
Not. Win. Wars.

AFTERNOON OF SMALL FAVORS

We didn't discuss the Accords that ended
The new country's war or the customs
Union across the pond that we'd not
Cross again but in which the school
Children of one of the parties hurled
Rocks to stop the rubber bullets of
Another's army between barricades
Blocking the streets of that old walled city
It was a bright January day unseasonably
Warm and we were happy
To share what we could

OVER THE LINE

Impending doom prepares a man to be prepared
One moment your Garanimals match up fine
The next you're circling species collapse

It's good to keep essentials close at hand
Grist for the body, manna for the mind
These things we take to be self-evident

Shelter offers its own state of the union
Justice requires the surrender of agency
Greater good gets lost in a crowd

Of conventional wisdom
Get your sixty seconds run
From each unforgiving sprint

Blow your own smoke
They can't take that away
Nor your illegal smile

AEGIS

Soft-bodied multi-limbed
Bilaterally symmetric I have
Learned to change my shape
Fit in small gaps and adapt
To those around I display
Surprising intelligence
Guile at survival
Turn me and I
Show you-you

ENLIGHTENMENT

Wave water what festival
       of atonement these sacred games
Boys in laughter hailing the roar
       the breakers pounding over coral
sand to sea wind-walking
             we cannot measure our place
in this world without disturbance
(the swell and the souse)   the courage
Of yes. To Life!

DENTED UNIVERSE

Is it the point
The shadow
The angle of
The bow
Or is it
You

FRIENDSHIP

Look at the size of you
Vast towards my want
And I feeling no shame

The softer self we carry
Within untangles all
The mind would bind

Remember this:
Bodies need feeding

SLIPSTREAM

We push forth from the sand
Sail the mantle of the lake

To be without destination
Sometimes the greatest gift

Is simple. Watch
The ripples not the oar.

A FAR PORTRAIT

Blessed peace this
Coca Cola contentment
No clothes but those
And feet to carry the view
Thru panoramic panes
Passed by from another
Side of the street

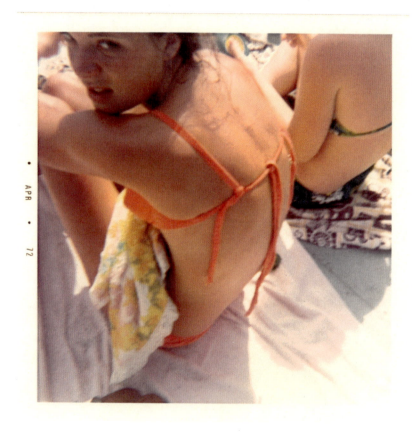

APPOLONIA 16

Drinking Tang in the sawdust

Row upon row beside the citrus grove

En Guarde! Sugar cane defeats beet root

Frantic for the roseate spoonbill's return

Ding Ding deserves another darling

From the children of the moon landing

Sunshine you are surrounded by stringed victory

Be my orange crush the bluest of marbles

OVERHEARD

Angels galloped beneath my apron

But this business of war does not stop

Nor strangers in the street

Perfectly we are burning rings

Each circles a hot new star

You may have your horses back

CHALICE

Is tragedy really a matter of imitation?

Animals make the language of their prey

Elaborations on a call note descanted

And of comedy whipped as wind through a basket

Caressing the nest or breathless in delight

The sun has sipped our wine

Sleeves paper the wall

FIDELITY OF CLOCKS

Among the glaciers and the rocks
Between the comings and the left
Bodies forgotten forget but really
Never do (how I miss you) stop ticking

DARING YOUNG MAN

Because you know there is no bottom
Like a fear that catches itself in the act
Of surrender, do sigh when you take me
In mad deflection I will swing forever
Knees wrapped to resist inhibition
Everything I cannot lie upon grows
Meshy at the thought before that
Secret leap is caught

BREAKERS

Just as you levitate

Consequential extras

Assemble into objects

My desire too has turned

As the stainless action of the waves

Never stop their hollow beckoning

So we bury our skin in the friction

COMPADRES

He pigeon-thumbed
The steering wheel
Drummed straight
As dust scattered
In the rearview mirrors
He remembers her
Feet keeping time
With the tin cans
Their wordless
Conversation
Filled the tank
At every turn
Hug the road
Right open

DEEP SONG

    A photographer in Denmark catches starlings in flight
an image like the glove of a boxer   time-tracked
                      in the unclasped act
of transverse and longitudinal motion   hits me
    como olas con plumas
        if waves wore feathers
           I could also see
woman incurved   her shoulder-turned torso
    so slim   somehow   we know
    she is young   can still love   her body
Danes call the murmuration a black sun   *un soleil noir*
    aerial time seems to cease
    this far north in the imperishable dusk of early autumn
        a juddering reminds we are near and nearly sky-same
predation may pulse the pattern
                perhaps a falcon or hawk has arrived
    a flying outward   or angling back   towards the fear
a cavity formed   canticles — *dyb sang*
    the rhythm of birds, the natural music of black poplars, of waves
                      look at the size of you

LAMMIX & THE RAJAH BROOKS

Born in the shade of rubber trees
You brushed away the bolts of grey war
To regard the emerald phantoms of the rainforest
Clustering birdwing butterflies with scarlet bands
As symbols of rarity and safe transport, your personal
Mythology locked in those darkly searching eyes:
In animal embrace. And now your daughter writes
These lines to say she has learned how they peel
With care a thin layer of bark in a downward spiral
To tap the milky fluid, moving to the other side,
To allow for healing and collection, new growth.

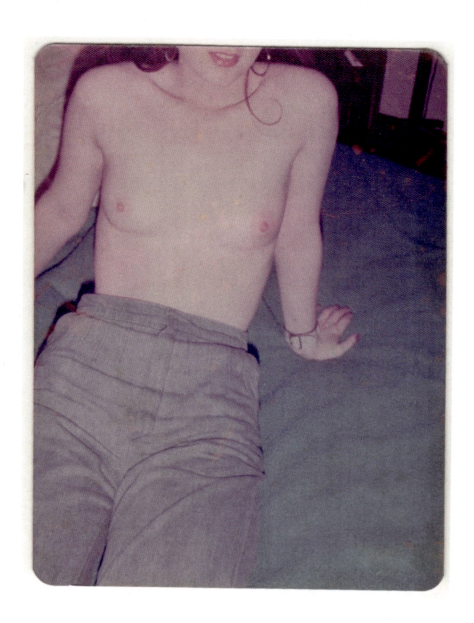

NOT MYSELF GOES HOME TO MYSELF

We are closer
Than the world
Between us even
The pressure of
Your eyes finds
Us both as alive
Ever searching

Tamsin Spencer Smith, at work

Tamsin Spencer Smith was born in England and lives in San Francisco. She's published three collections of poetry, *Word Cave* (RiskPress Foundation), *Between First and Second Sleep* (FMSBW), and *Displacement Geology* (FMSBW), in addition to a novel, *XISLE* (FMSBW). Smith is also a painter, exhibiting with the Divers Gallery. She frequently writes about art and has contributed to several catalogue essays for artists including Zio Ziegler, Joan Brown, and Hollis Heichimer. Smith holds an MA from The Fletcher School at Tufts University and a BA from Kenyon College, where she graduated *summa cum laude* with highest honors in English for her thesis on Vladimir Nabokov.

Matt Gonzalez is a native of McAllen, Texas who has been living in California since 1987. He obtained a BA from Columbia University and JD from Stanford Law School. He has been collecting found photography for over a decade and has written for various art publications including *Juxtapoz, San Francisco Arts Quarterly,* and *Ceramics: Art and Perception.*

THE DIVERS COLLECTION

Number 1
Hôtel des Étrangers, poems by **Joachim Sartorius**
translated from German to English by **Scott J. Thompson**

Number 2
Making Art, a memoir by **Mary Julia Klimenko**

Number 3
XISLE, a novel by **Tamsin Spencer Smith**

Number 4
Famous Dogs of the Civil War, a novel by **Ben Dunlap**

Number 5
Now Let's See What You're Gonna Do by **Katerina Gogou**
translated from Greek to English by **A.S.**
with an introduction by **Jack Hirschman**

Number 6
Sunshine Bell / The Autobiography of a Genius,
an annotated edition by **Ben Dunlap**

Number 7
The Profound M, poems by **Tamsin Spencer Smith**
with an introduction by **Matt Gonzalez**

Made in the USA
Columbia, SC
10 July 2021